I0158276

Renaissance of the Psyche

Renaissance of the Psyche was published by Hampton Publishing

House, LLC P.O. Box 29001 Columbus, Ohio 43229 Copyright © 2017 by Melica Niccole

All rights reserved. This book may not be reproduced in any manner without the written consent from the publisher.

Library of Congress Control Number: 2017959981

ISBN 978-0-9976875-3-8

Printed in the United States of America

Dedicated to those who want a little more than the usually. The usually is easy to get but does not challenge you to get back up and push harder when you fall.

Table of Contents

- Mind
- Smile
- Finish Line
- They Say...
- Table
- Nina Simone's Black Birds
- The Moon and the Sun
- We The People
- When Forever Ends Tomorrow
- Ahead of My Time
- The Shawshank Before the Redemption

Respect

I have to give respect where respect is due
This poetry thing has never been new
The greats before us paved the way for us
To lyrically flow and make a stand for us
We have to pay homage to the present and past
Because it's with past that our presence last See
Nikki Giovanni was an active poet
Created different platforms for others to show it
Sonya Sanchez is world renowned
The love of language created beautiful sound
Edgar Allan Poe, the father of detective stories
The Raven was where he got his glory
Maya Angelou said "Still I Rise."
Phenomenal Woman with her Eyes on the Prize
William Ernest Henley was a delectable soul
Master of his fate and captain of his soul
Amiri Baraka fought for the rights of his own
Poet, playwright, and very well-known
Sam Walter Foss wrote The House by the Side of
the Road
Listening to that poem will never get old
Etheridge Knight did Poems from Prison
And this is where his name had risen
Gwendolyn Brooks won the Pulitzer Prize
highly influential and very wise
See these are the greats who we must
acknowledge
And this right here is why we pay homage

Paralyzing People's Minds (Inspired by Freedom Time by Lauryn Hill)

Paralyzing people's minds
Leaving them blind
For their third eye they could not find
Slightly confused
Souls banished and bruised
Thinking they're the winners
When misconstrued wins often lose
It's time for an awakening
Enlighten your mind
And do away with all the verbal and physical
hating
Free your mind and let your soul relax in
comfort
Live by your word and create no more
discomfort.

I Miss You

I miss you
And I really do not even know you
My spirit wants to vibe
And flow with you
Free style together
And go toe to toe with you
Travel to a distant land
And cuddle with you
I just want to hold you
Our bodies come together
And create a mold of you
Singing Back to life
Soul II Soul with you
Kick off your shoes and relate your feet Xscape
with you
Ain't no mountain high Marvin Gaye and
Tammi Terrell with you
I want to fly with you
Giggle and act shy with you
Laugh a thousand laughs with you
Sit on the porch and.... Reminisce
But I guess I'm infatuated
Elated
Vastly gaited
Emotions precipitated
So let me slow it down and say...
Hello...
How's your day...
You good...
Goodbye

A Tribute to Nina Simone (Eunice Kathleen Waymon)

To be young, gifted, and black
Mind's tribulations
Not wanting to be misunderstood
Love her, leave her, or let her be lonely
Nina's depression deteriorated her slowly
Entrance into Curtis Institute of Music in
Philadelphia denied
Because of a color that she just could not hide
Pain bellowed inside of her mind
Mental health was the issue
A diagnosis
Not at the time
Sweet little Eunice
Wherefore art thou so sad?
Did success not pull up to your driveway
And place you in the driver's seat?
Did love not bruise and batter your soul?
Did children not enter your womb
And produce a healthy baby girl?
Maybe it was the fact of being misunderstood
Understood on the stage
But forgotten in the crowd
I say
Live on Nina Through your beautiful music that
continues to play even after your death in 2003 Live
on Nina

Love's Utopia

You are the feeling that burns deep inside of me
This flame Engulfs me
Red surges of vibrant feelings
Orange shavings of lover's lane dealings
Let us get lost
Lost in each other's soul
Lost to the point of no control
I have placed my love on cruise control
This is something I thought you should know
Let my love Marinate in your spirit
If love was a performance evaluation
You would receive the highest merit
This place is too perfect to stay away from
My love I just want to give you more than some
Take All of me
My pain relieves
All of a suddenly
Joy cannot be Dystopia
For I have gone to Love's Utopia

Living for the love of...

I am living for the love of ...
Love
Living for the warmth and kindness it exudes
Living for the smiles
The truth it expels
The encouragement it gives off
Love embraces my soul
Allows me to keep moving forward
It encourages me to be better
Helps me to see my faults
Because love is imitated
Duplicated
And sometimes Taught

I Dream in Love

Some people dream in pictures
While other people dream in colors
I dream in love

The Truth Will Set You Free

Let freedom ring
Let birdies sing
Let Autumn Spring
Let true men king
Let leaders lead
Let the scholarly read
Let liars take heed
Because the truth will set you free
Let these vibes flow
Let the unknown be known
Let hawks scour
Let less than men cower
Let the imposters relinquish their power
Let the giants tower
Because... The truth will set you free

Liars

The scrum of the earth
Their words
They know not who they hurt
Trust
No at all
For these liars
Always fall

Long Live the Poet

Long live the poet
Filled with words
Spoken truths
Fabled fairies
Stories galore
When it rains
It pours
Sweet
But never half past four
Glutton woes
Rhythmic flows
Donner's Blitzen
A cookout fixin'
Truth of tales
All else pales
The Poet's remorse
Different from its source

Music

Music fills my soul with pleasant melodies
Poetically flowing to the rhythmic vibrations in my
Ear
I hear nothing
But Caribbean vibes
Drums bellowing to the musical genius
Inside
I hear the long
Exaggerated guitar that pulls the cords in a bluesy
direction of freedom and
Pain
Can you hear people uniting and parading their
love?
They are fearless
They are ready for peace and love
I imagine Woodstock 1969
Circles of people
Different cultures
Holding hands
Bringing harmony to Dr. Martin Luther King, Jr's
I have a dream speech
Does music fill your soul?
Does it create a connection between you and I?
Forget a ride or die
Ready to die mentality with a ready to live capability
What's the point of dying
If you don't even know what you're riding for?
So, ride to this music
And learn to live for what you were willing to die for

Dream

Let us
Fantasize of a world of dreams
Be on the same
Mission
While eating ice cream
Let us be about our business and uplift each other
Hug
And embrace one another
Can we use empathy in our interactions?
Smile and act like we are old fashioned
Let us love like our life
Depended on it
Help and be open-minded
Let us do more than just talk
We can work together
And become the
Dream Team

Park of Life

You breathe life into me
Awaken my glow
Bring life into an idled soul
Smelling of fresh algae
Pine early in the morning
Glistening water
With the sun perched
In a water ripple
Flowing constantly
In a pool of possibilities
If I was a fish in your pond
I'd splish, splash
Taking water in my mouth
And releasing it as
I fly on the top of the pond
Flying
Smiling and coming to a complete stop mid-air
I would then graciously go back into the pond
Happier than when I first started
Splish, splashing
And doing the same thing all over again
But I'm not a fish
So, I will imagine a life complete
Enjoying the everyday life
Of a park inhabited at the
Park of Life

Sun

Beautiful
Golden
Never ending
Un-cloned
Remarkable
Peaceful
Happiness
Beaches
Summer Solstice
Ice Cream Trucks
Slip and slides
Amusement Park rides none less the wise...
My sunshine

Broken Fences

Broken fences
Feelings tensing
Scattered feelings
Endings turn into beginnings

Omen

Blinded by sight
Deafened with words
An omen brought me back to life
For I was disturbed
Love lied to me
Blindsided me
Ripped my wounds
And departed just as soon
I tried to pick up the pieces
But something inside of me was deceasing
Maggot infested heart
Punctured to the core
Only thing to save me was to love no more

King Triton's Wrath

Have you ever felt the wrath of King Triton?
Down in the depths of the ocean
Where Ursula hands out to-be-what-I-want potion
Where Mer-people reside
And they don't have to go inside to hide
Red eyes glowing
Illuminated Trident showing
Heart pounding
Teeth
Gritting
Greek
God throne sitting
Son of Poseidon and Amphitrite
Killer of Misenus
Battling him would be a risk
But none of you are really
Hearing this
Slayer
Nominated himself as the mayor
Never challenge him because
He'll leave you without a prayer
He'll protect his daughters
With all of his might
And then banish someone
Out of sight
But that's just the good Ole' King
He'll make Ariel sniffle, smile, and sing!

Losing Myself

I'm lost
Nowhere to turn
This shit burns
But not for you to discern

Butterflies

I'm getting butterflies
Down in the depths of my soul
Because there has been a reawakening
I had been sleeping
For way too long
It was time
Time for me to get UP!
And assert myself
Time for me to let the caterpillar
Become the butterfly
It was time
Time for me to rise

Body

Lay your body into mine
Metamorphosize
Spewing Maya Angelou's Still I Rise
You got me Hypnotized
Academic integrity
For you I'll plagiarize
Just to look
Into your eyes
Please tell me
No more lies
Because for you
I'll compromise
Can't you see
Don't ask why
I am who I am
Don't take me off
This high

No sunshine

Only pillars of salty roads
Corrosion crusted cars
And phones with no connection bars

A Belt Made of Chastity (Promise Ring)

Promises
Venus's girdle
Untied with Cinthia's virtue
Commitment
Marie de France
Myths
Truths
And all the mistruths
Society
Thoughts on love
Condemning
Protecting
Saving a piece for later
Women
12 century
Opened with force
But only untied by lovers
Belts Chasity Belts of Chasity A promise ring

Brilliant

I've witnessed
Brilliant imposters
Claiming to be something they're not
Their words say, "I'm your gal."
While their eyes tell a different story
Are you a Brilliant Imposter?

I Dwell In Possibility Too! (A response to Emily Dickinson)

You dwell in Possibility?
Well, I do Too!
Our thoughts somewhat similar
Who really knew?
You dwell in Possibility
A fairer House than Prose
I dwell in Creativity
Embodied by a White and Blue rose
Your chambers made of Cedar
With an everlasting roof
My chambers made of silk linens
With imaginations of fun, friends, and little dog
woofs
Your hands spread wide
To gather Paradise
Paradise is within me
As well as love, sweet, and a pinch of nice

Captain (Inspired by William Ernest Henley)

How do we inspire ourselves to greatness
When nothing else will do?
Do we cherish each moment
And uplift the love from you?
We are captains, but we truly know
You are the master of the wind
Without you
Our beginning would become the end
Like William once stated I am the master of my fate
I am the captain of my soul
Meaning I am a leader
From the black pit
From pole to pole
Bloody head
Never stopped me
Diligent
Watch me
Night
Covers
Horror
Shade
My body
Unafraid

Lose Control

My spirit yearns to live carelessly
To be free
And live justly
But we all know those characteristics Are
sometimes hard to achieve
So all I can do is hope Wish
And believe

All I see is the possibilities

I will not confirm to what you want me to be
I will not shy away from what was intended of me
But rather reform to what I need to be
I cannot allow people to take my victory
My dreams and passion will make history
If only you could see what I see
Then you would know why I am ME!

Emotional Tundra

My emotional tundra
Is more vernacular than Mumbra
And more spectacular than Sandra

Anticipation

I anticipate
Seeing your dark caressing eyes
Massaging my thoughts
With blissful conversations
That leads to long walks
In summer's night's garden
The forbidden fruit
I'm tempted
Not by a serpent
Or a soldier of the slither
But by my magnetic attraction
That has declared
Not to repel your charismatic spirit
Words
Which populates a mouthful of let's
Because at one point in time
Those let's were I
Because I was the only person
That I needed to take care of
This feeling I've tried to disguise
With "why are you here?"
I ask this question
Because your presence
Makes my mind venture to places
Unbeknown to travelers
Who try to sky dive
Without a parachute
It's called
Love free falling
Because my love comes at no cost to you
The only debt you owe
Is the restitution of your soul
Your soul deserves to be loved
To the point of no control
Your body seeks to enjoy long walks
In the park
Singing in the rain

While gazing at the sky for entertainment
Did I ever tell you
I anticipate seeing your dark caressing eyes?

Drifting

I sit here Drifting
Drifting to a place
Like no other
Where people express themselves openly
Without the fear of
Repercussions
Drift with me
Do You Know Me?

Do you know me?

Our paths cross
Like a clock that strikes 12pm each day
While a tornado siren sounds
Because today marks
Wednesday afternoon
Though we came into contact many times
Ate with the same friends
Sang the same songs
And laughed at the same jokes
We were worlds apart
Though we were worlds apart
We sat staring at each other for 15 years
15 minutes, which felt like
15 long and intense years
I listened as chronic cries of help
Spilled from your lungs
In the form of emotional pitfalls
Which pierces my ears
Like screeching tires on wet cement
Non-judgmental to the attack trumpets
That blared from the instrument
While disassembling the key notes
That played a vital role
In the player's beautifully organized melody Though
the melodies were not as perfect as intended
They were committed to the same performance
The same song
And the same uniqueness
You wanted conformity
All melodies and notes should sound
And look the same
Therefore, everyone recognize them as the same
I sat stunned as the new sound
Puffed through your cheeks
Was intended to be glorifying
Yet left a lasting impression of
"Are you serious?"

On the tongues of those
Who heard the horrendous tune
Shimming out of your lips
I witness
A trumpet
In search of true identity
Playing softly
While recognizing itself as a Saxophone
A trumpet
That takes heed in making itself stand tall While
walking distastefully on top of other cohorts
That were once held to the same standard Knowing
our imbalance to common life discussions
I rethink my original questions and say
Do you know me?

Love

Two bodies
One heart
A magnetic attraction
As beautiful as art
Feeding off each other
And releasing energy into the universe
Showing the world
The way love should be dispersed
The artist Produces the most beautiful brush
strokes ever
Showing off his talents
Of being creative and cleaver

Monstrosity

Who created this monstrosity you say?
I say you did
And you did it your way
Your opinions
Your actions
And your thoughts created this
Now looking at your creation
Is something you will miss?

Mind

I want to caress your cerebellum
Massage your medulla oblongata
Love you long time
Because your love is hotter than "wata"
Travel to the depths of your soul
While peeling back your fears
Embrace your spirit
And catch every single tear
I want to curve your appetite
Connect with you on some many levels
Get close to your spirit
In which I revel
Best friend qualifies
Your mind astonishes me
Serene for which we be

Finish Line

I started out like a tortoise
Walking at a pace
Which seemed to be
Slower than nails
I often questioned myself
Will I ever prevail?
Will I reach the finish line of success?
Which seemed to be
Thousands of miles away
Knowing what I knew
I gave it my all anyway

They say...

They say
Life is what you make it
When opportunities come
You better take it
And like acting
You cannot fake it
And the feeling you hold deep inside
Never forsake it
They also say
Horus' eye is the enemy
And displaying the rainbow is a sin to me
But if we were made not to judge
Why do we condemn our brother and hold a
grudge?
Why do we talk about others in the wrong?
And not realize it's a mistake of our own
Love our neighbors with all our heart
Give to our children from the start
But that's just the beginning
Of what we can do
We can be who we were meant to be
And do what we need to do

The Table

I sit at the table
Of liberated minds
And unconditioned souls
Taking in the beautiful view
Of personalities unconstraint
It's like sitting on the edge of your windowsill With
your feet dangling down
And the world at your feet
Only I Dream speeches
And truth society teaches
Could have imagined
Such a beautiful event
The table of liberated minds
And unconditioned souls

Words

Words
Nina Simone's Black birds
Kicked to the curb
Without a word
Ya heard?

Chances
Second glances
Flawed circumstances
Unspoken
To the spoken ransoms

Snakes
Acting fake
What a waste
Piercing eyes
Glistening skies
With them souls that hate

He said
She said
Blah, blah said
We said
Let's lay the said to bed

Peaceful words
You gotta fly black bird
Respect to this, that, and the third

Words
Birds
Nina Simone's
Black Birds

The Moon and the Sun

I want to look into your eyes
And get lost in the moon
Die in ecstasy
Because my soul will be rebirthed soon
Travel to a distant land
Where your heart captures mine
Kiss until the sun comes up
And hope we don't run out of time
I want to live in your confidence
Cast off your fears
Be your co-captain Boy,
I will let you steer
I want our minds to meet
Catching the rhyme
Never missing a beat
Like SWV I get so weak
Weak in the knees
Weak in the feet
But that's just astronomy
Got to be biology
Mixed with a little physiology
Don't forget the splash of psychology

We the People

We the people
In order to form a more perfect union of hatred,
pain, and suffering
Take away your inalienable rights (Justice)
Take away all things that are viable (Domestic
Tranquility)
Create unnecessary international nemesis
(Common defense)
Relinquish all your rights (General welfare)
Say everyone is free
While putting restrictions on groups (Liberty)
See
We the people
Didn't mean all people
Clearly it only meant the select few
The select who could interrupt the law
To what they wanted it to be
The select few who could make the just look
unjust in a matter of moments
We the people
Is constitutionally a misrepresentation of what
"we" is suppose to mean

When Forever Ends Tomorrow

Sometimes forever ends tomorrow
Leaving no permanent casualties
Only hurt feelings
And temporary states of mind
Forever is sometimes spoken
As to mean until the end of time
Or the end of our lifetime
We as people know
That our forever is sometimes overshadowed
By beautiful spoken soliloquies
With no partakers of this relational truce
Our forever ends unequivocally
Giving rise to a whole new meaning of forever
I say
Live forever with as much enthusiasm as possible
Because forever could one day
Be true to its inception

Ahead of My Time

Sometimes I feel I'm ahead of my time Waiting for
others to catch up Brain catches anxiety attacks
and won't let up People consult me on a regular
about decisions Wanting me to give them advice
any my vision Some things they can't hear Because
they don't listen Then come back with strife
Because something is missing Life all out of control
With no mission Love strayed away Just too much
tension When will we learn And go down the
straight and narrow Did we not learn from all them
Kings and pharaohs Giving people the side eye
Like it's the new ish Big dreams like were a big
whale When were a little fish Out of the water
Trying so very hard to catch our breath Depleting
our funds 'Til there's nothing left But that's just my
flo And how it really goes Leaving you with a few
things That you should know

The Shawshank Before the Redemption

Shattered windows
Shattered dreams
Ulterior motives it seems
Pieces of him
Pieces of me
It's just too bad the blind is the first to see
Legacies undone
A man gone before the sun
Set on his life
Fatherless kids gloom amongst the ranks
Souls torn for they have witnessed the
Shawshank before the redemption
It's sad because some may never get this
The past remains the present with heavily coated
makeup
Covering up all the blemishes
Showing the beautiful exterior
When it's the interior that is
"Still under construction"
Keep out and skull bone signs show there is
imminent danger,
But how can one know when the package has
been adorned to protect?

The Good Ole' Days

In thinking about my childhood days, I really must thank my mother and fathers for making me who I am today. There are certain memories that I cherish and hold dear to my heart about them. One fond memory I have of my mother is how she dedicated her time and effort to clean up our community. My mother swept the sidewalks and picked up paper that people had so uncaringly thrown on the ground. Her actions motivated me to want to do the same things. She was my role model, who I looked up to and wanted to be like. Another memory of my mother that I admired was her ability to get along with everyone, even when it was evident that there was no relational connection. She forgave easily and did not let herself be engulfed in the negativity of others. Today, I am still a work in progress, taking in all the things my mother did and making some of her actions my own. As for my fathers, they taught me how to be quiet in the mist of loudness. They showed me that not every comment deserves a response, and some responses could be incorrect. I was also shown that silence is golden in the most chaotic situations. I still practice the characteristic of controlling my tongue for I know emotions have a way of altering the way people respond. My parents taught me how to be independent of my own thoughts. They taught me that I could really rely on one person and that was myself. This is the very reason that I work hard because I know that I only have me. While this may seem sad to some, it's reality. We all should work as if we only have ourselves to rely on or kids if we are blessed to have them. This way we would not expect certain things or get our feelings hurt by expecting these things to be given to us Be optimist when it comes to lessons and life.

My LIFE

When I think of My Life, Mary J. Blidge's second album released in 1994 comes in mind. Songs like, "You Bring me Joy", "You Gotta Believe", and "No One Else". This is exactly how I feel about my life. My joy is through my passion. I am extremely happy with my events, books, and success. I have been afforded so many opportunities in relocating to New Jersey that I cannot be upset with any negative things that have taken place to get me to where I am now. Believing is a skill to help people believe in themselves and the things they can accomplish. I am currently a Supported Education Specialist, which is like being a Career Counselor. I assist individuals 18 years of age and older with identifying if a higher education degree is right for them. Once this has been established, I then assist them with completing the application requirements, getting into school, and maintaining school. It is truly amazing watching these individuals go from being unsure about themselves to believing in their skills and abilities. I am truly thankful to be able to assist other individuals and help them identify their wants, needs, passions, and go after their dreams.

Thank GOD!

No one else will replace my continued connection and love with the Almighty and His continued strength and guidance in my life. There is truly no one like Him. He continues to strengthen me and make me better than I was yesterday. I truly thank him for blessing me and making me determined to succeed. There is no love better or stronger then His. I ask Him to continue to bless the lives of my family, friends, acquaintances, and those who truly need His help. Remember, don't just go to Him about your needs. Go to Him about your accomplishments, waking up each morning, and just being the person, you are today. Through Him, you will see the truth.

Resources

Nikki Giovanni
http://www.biography.com/people/nikki-giovanni9312272#popular-poetry Accessed 7/10/17

Sonya Sanchez
http://www.theblackscholar.org/board/sanchez/ Accessed 7/10/17

Sonya Sanchez
https://www.poetryfoundation.org/poems-andpoets/poets/detail/sonia-sanchez Accessed 7/10/17

Edgar Allan Poe
http://www.biography.com/people/edgar-allanpoe-9443160#synopsis Accessed 7/10/17

William Ernest Henley
https://www.poetryfoundation.org/poems-andpoets/poets/detail/william-ernest-henley Accessed 7/12/17

Amiri Baraka http://www.amiribaraka.com/ Accessed 7/15/17

Sam Walter Foss
https://www.alsintl.com/resources/poetry/thehouse-by-the-side-of-the-road/ Accessed 7/15/17

Etheridge Knight
https://www.poetryfoundation.org/poems-andpoets/poets/detail/etheridge-knight Accessed 8/12/17

Gwendolyn Brooks
https://www.poetryfoundation.org/poems-
andpoets/poets/detail/gwendolyn-brooks
Accessed 8/12/17

Laurn Hill (It's Freedom Time)
https://www.youtube.com/watch?v=peS99vRe
Vwg

Nina Simone What Happended, Miss Simone
(2015)- Netflix.

Little Mermaid (1989)- Movie.

Emily Dickinson
https://www.poetryfoundation.org/poems/52197
/i -dwell-in-possibility-466 Accessed 8/12/17

Marie De France- Chastity Belt
http://ww/w.semmelweis.museum.hu/muzeum/
kia llitasok/erenyov/reszletes_en.html
Accessed 8/12/17 Proof

www.ingramcontent.com/pod-product-compliance
Lightning Source LLC
Chambersburg PA
CBHW021919040426
42448CB00007B/825